Julia Holt

Published in association with The Basic Skills Agency

Hodder Murray

A MEMBER OF THE HODDER HEADLINE GROUP

The Publishers would like to thank the following for permission to reproduce copyright material:

Photo credits
p.2 © Shane Partridge/Rex Features; p.7 © Harry Goodwin/Rex Features; p.10 © Rex Features; p.15 © Neal Preston/Corbis; p.19 © Tess Peni/Rex Features; p.21 © Mirek Towski/Rex Features; p.24 © Stewart Cook/Rex Features.

Orders: please contact Bookpoint Ltd, 130 Milton Park, Abingdon, Oxon OX14 4SB. Telephone (44) 01235 827720. Fax: (44) 01235 400454. Lines are open from 9.00–6.00, Monday to Saturday, with a 24-hour message answering service. Visit our website at www.hoddereducation.co.uk

Copyright © Julia Holt 2005
First published in 2005 by
Hodder Murray, a member of the Hodder Headline Group
338 Euston Road
London NW1 3BH

Impression number   10 9 8 7 6 5 4 3 2
Year   2010 2009 2008 2007 2006 2005

Cover photo © Neal Preston/Corbis
Typeset in 14pt Palatino by SX Composing DTP, Rayleigh, Essex.
Printed in Great Britain by CPI Bath.

A catalogue record for this title is available from the British Library

ISBN-10 0 340 90062 8
ISBN-13 978 0 340 90062 8

Contents

1 Beware of the Owner!

There is a house in Beverly Hills
and on the gate it says:

> **Never mind the dog
> beware of the owner**

The family who live in the house
are like no other family in the world.
They don't look like anyone else
and they don't live like anyone else.
Yet lots of people want to live with them.
They are the Osbournes.

The Osbournes' house in Beverly Hills, Los Angeles.

The Osbournes' house is a mix of Gothic
and very ordinary things.
There are crosses and skulls everywhere
but there are also flowery curtains.

There is a dead bat in the bathroom
but they also have a pool and a giant screen TV.

The house is very different and so are the animals.
And then there is the family…

2 Ozzy

In 1948, at the end of World War II,
England was a bleak place.
There wasn't much food in the Osbourne house
and there were no luxuries.
Six children shared one bed.

This was the world
that John Osbourne was born into.
As a teenager, his one dream was to get rich
and be in a band like The Beatles.

At school John was good at two things –
singing and making the other kids laugh.
They called him Ozzy.

Ozzy left school at 15 and he started a band.
They didn't make much money.
So sometimes Ozzy went into people's gardens
and dug up their vegetables to eat.
Sometimes he had no shoes to wear.

He tried lots of jobs
but they didn't make him rich.
So he turned to crime.
He became a burglar.
But the police caught him and he was sent to jail.

Ozzy came out of jail
with the first of his many tattoos.
He had 'OZZY' on his knuckles
and a smiley face on each knee.

In 1967, Ozzy was still looking
for a band to sing with.
He got together with three friends from school.

Then, after two years of practising
and nearly starving, Black Sabbath was born.
They were one of the very first heavy metal bands.
They took their name from a horror film.
Finally, in 1970, they got a recording contract.
They made their first album.

Ozzy was paid £50 for his work on the album.
He got himself a pair of shoes
and went home to show the album to his mum.

In five years, Black Sabbath
became mega-stars and mega-rich.
By 1975, Ozzy had a farm in England
and two children with his first wife, Thelma.

Black Sabbath: Ozzy is on the left.

But Ozzy had worked non-stop for five years
and he had taken a lot of drugs.
His lifestyle was killing him.
Thelma couldn't stand it. She left him.

Ozzy needed to make some changes.
So in 1979 he left Black Sabbath
and he formed a new band.
He also met Sharon and she became his manager.
He says that she saved his life.

With Sharon as his manager,
Ozzy became famous all over again.

He became famous for doing crazy things,
like biting the head off a bat.
Ozzy thought the bat was a toy
thrown on to the stage.
He had to have a course of rabies shots
afterwards.

By the time he was 50, Ozzy and his family
were said to be worth £40 million.

Today Ozzy lives a millionaire lifestyle.
He has homes in Beverly Hills and in England.
His dream of getting away from poverty
has come true.
He is older and happier
and he doesn't bite the heads off
small animals any more.

Sharon Osbourne.

3 The Show

'The Osbournes' TV show
started life in October 2001.
Sharon agreed a fee of £200,000.

Twelve MTV cameras moved in to start filming
just as the family moved in
to their new house in Beverly Hills.

The first series of 'The Osbournes'
started with them unpacking in their new house.
They unpacked some boxes marked 'PANS'
and others marked 'DEVIL'S HEADS'
and 'DEAD THINGS'.

'The Osbournes' was one of the first
reality TV shows.
The camera crew filmed the family
for four months 24/7.
The only rule was no filming in the bedrooms
or the bathrooms.
Also, the oldest girl, Aimee,
chose not to be filmed.
She moved into a flat near the house.

The show was an instant success
with fans of all ages.
More people watched 'The Osbournes'
than any other MTV show.
They liked the craziest family on TV.

Behind all their craziness
is a family who clearly love one another.
The Osbournes are really close.

In the show Ozzy shuffles round the house
in make-up and black clothes.

4 Sharon

Today Sharon has three jobs.
She is Ozzy's manager and she is Ozzy's wife.
She is also mum to Aimee, Kelly and Jack.
None of these jobs is easy!

Sharon says that she is a workaholic.
She only needs four hours' sleep a night.
She set up 'The Osbournes' TV show.
She has had her own chat show.
Every year she runs a 30-city, heavy metal tour.
It's called 'Ozzfest' and Ozzy is the star.

Now she has a new show in England.
It's called 'The X Factor'
and it's a talent show for singers and bands.

His long hair is tied back
and his arms are tattooed.
Almost every word he says is a swear word.

He is still the wild man of rock
but he is also a typical dad.
He is confused by his kids
and by the modern world.
He can't change a bin liner or work the TV remote.
But to lots of kids, Ozzy and Sharon
are their dream parents.

Four series of 'The Osbournes'
have put millions of dollars
into the family's bank account.
The last show was filmed in June 2004.

'The Osbournes' was one of the first
reality TV shows.
The camera crew filmed the family
for four months 24/7.
The only rule was no filming in the bedrooms
or the bathrooms.
Also, the oldest girl, Aimee,
chose not to be filmed.
She moved into a flat near the house.

The show was an instant success
with fans of all ages.
More people watched 'The Osbournes'
than any other MTV show.
They liked the craziest family on TV.

Behind all their craziness
is a family who clearly love one another.
The Osbournes are really close.

In the show Ozzy shuffles round the house
in make-up and black clothes.

3 The Show

'The Osbournes' TV show
started life in October 2001.
Sharon agreed a fee of £200,000.

Twelve MTV cameras moved in to start filming
just as the family moved in
to their new house in Beverly Hills.

The first series of 'The Osbournes'
started with them unpacking in their new house.
They unpacked some boxes marked 'PANS'
and others marked 'DEVIL'S HEADS'
and 'DEAD THINGS'.

Sharon and Ozzy at their wedding in 1982.

In 2000, Sharon took a look
at herself in the mirror.
She wanted to change.
So she spent £120,000 on cosmetic surgery.
She also lost 50 kilos (nearly 8 stone).
Sharon is now listed as one of the most
beautiful women in the world.

In 2002, Sharon was struck down by cancer.
Doctors said that she had
a one in three chance of living
but she is all clear now.
When Ozzy found out that she was better,
he threw a big party.

At the party Sharon and Ozzy got married again.
The first time was 20 years before, in Hawaii.
The second time was in a Beverly Hills hotel,
in front of MTV cameras and lots of friends.

5 Kelly

Kelly and Jack take after their dad.
They swear a lot and they share
his love of heavy metal music.

The day after Kelly was born in 1984,
Ozzy booked himself into a clinic to dry out.
He stayed sober for a few months
but soon went back to his crazy ways.
And that's the world that Kelly grew up in.

She grew up in England, but in 1997
the family moved to the USA to live.
They kept a house in England
but only for holidays.
Kelly was 13 and she had to
get used to living in LA.

Kelly hated school.
She was dyslexic and she found school hard.
Ozzy told her not to worry.
Going round the world with him
gave her a different kind of schooling.
She left school at 16.

Since then Kelly has tried being a model.
She has also started a career in music.
Her first single was a re-make of
Madonna's 'Papa Don't Preach'.
In 2002, she recorded her first album.
Ozzy is very proud of Kelly's success.

Kelly's next plan is to act.
She is filming a TV series in Canada.
It's called 'Life As We Know It'.

Kelly's career is managed by one of the best
managers around – her mum Sharon!

Kelly Osbourne.

6 Jack

Just like Kelly,
Jack's school days were difficult.
He is dyslexic too.
Jack's problems are a big part of the TV show.

Sometimes he went to bed drunk at 4am
and slept until late afternoon.
We saw the nanny pick him up from school camp.
All he had done at the camp
was throw rocks at his teachers.

No one was shocked when Jack left school early.

Jack Osbourne.

Today Jack has been sober for over a year
and he has a job.
He is a music talent scout for his mum.
He travels around the USA
looking for the best young talent.
Then he plays their music to his mum.

The success of 'The Osbournes' TV show
has opened doors for both Kelly and Jack.
It has helped them both to find work.

7 The Rest of the Family

The Osbournes don't live on a farm
but they still have lots of animals.
They have three cats and six small dogs.
Then there is Lola. She is Jack's bulldog.
She is not house-trained!

All the animals make messes
and they drive Ozzy crazy.
He keeps saying, 'No more animals,'
but the family keep adopting more and more.

Rob is the latest family member.
He is the same age as Kelly
and he is her best friend.
His mum had cancer, like Sharon, but she died.
So the family have adopted him.
They call him Baby Osbourne.

Ozzy, Jack, Sharon, Kelly and Rob.

Last but not least, there is Melinda.
She is the family's nanny.
She is the one who holds the family together
and sorts out all the messes.

8 The Future

Sharon says there won't be any more
of 'The Osbournes' TV show.
She says that they have all grown up and moved on.
They are all doing new things.

Now Ozzy wants to get back
to how they were before MTV moved in.
He says, 'I want to have fun.
I don't want cameras following me 24/7.
I don't want to be the richest man
in the graveyard.'

Today the family is very rich and very famous.
Ozzy has met the Queen and President Bush.
The Osbournes have taken fame in their stride.
Behind all the craziness
the family can be very normal.
Whatever they do in the future
they will always stick together.

9 The Osbournes Quiz

1   What dead animal can you find in the
     Osbournes' bathroom?

2   When John Osbourne was young,
     what did he want to do?

3   What was the name of Ozzy Osbourne's
     first band?

4   Why did Ozzy bite the head off a bat?

5   When the Osbournes moved house,
     what was written on the packed boxes?

6   Which Osbourne chose not to be involved
     in the TV series?

7   How many hours' sleep does Sharon
     need each night?

8   What was the name of Kelly's first single?

9   What did Jack do at school camp?

10   How many animals do the Osbournes have?